Living in a Biome

Life in an Ocean
Revised Edition

by Carol K. Lindeen

Consulting Editor: Gail Saunders-Smith, Ph.D.

Consultant: Sandra Mather, Professor Emerita
Department of Geology and Astronomy, West Chester University
West Chester, Pennsylvania

CAPSTONE PRESS
a capstone imprint

Pebble Plus is published by Capstone Press
1710 Roe Crest Drive, North Mankato, Minnesota 56003
www.mycapstone.com

Library of Congress Cataloging-in-Publication Data is available on the Library of Congress website.
ISBN 978-1-5157-3693-6 (revised paperback)

Editorial Credits
Martha E. H. Rustad, editor; Kia Adams, designer and illustrator; Juliette Peters, cover production designer; Kelly Garvin, photo researcher;
Eric Kudalis, product planning editor

Photo Credits
Capstone Press: 7 Top; Digital Vision: 1, 13; iStockphoto: beusbeus, 17, Searsie, 15; Rubberball Productions: 5; Shutterstock: CyberEak, 9,
EpicStockMedia, 7 Bottom, KGrif, 21, Rich Carey, Cover, 19, Sean Lema, 11

Note to Parents and Teachers

The Living in a Biome series supports national science standards related to life science. This book describes and
illustrates animal and plant life in oceans. The photographs support early readers in understanding the text.
This book also introduces early readers to subject-specific vocabulary words, which are defined in the Glossary
section. Early readers may need assistance to read some words and to use the Table of Contents, Glossary, Read
More, Internet Sites, and Index/Word List sections of the book.

Word Count: 109
Early-Intervention Level: 12

Printed in the United States   5669

Table of Contents

What Are Oceans?

An ocean is a large, deep
body of salt water.

Oceans are found in every part of the world. The Pacific Ocean is the largest ocean.

Arctic Ocean

Atlantic Ocean

Pacific Ocean

Indian Ocean

N

W   E

S

Ocean Animals

Fish swim in oceans. They
eat small animals and plants.

Crabs have hard shells. Crabs walk on the ocean floor.

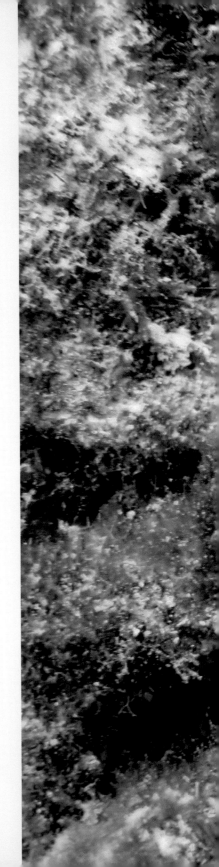

Sharks have fins and sharp
teeth. They hunt for fish
and crabs.

Ocean Plants

Seaweed is an ocean plant.

It grows near the shore.

Kelp is an ocean plant with long leaves. Fish can hide in kelp.

Sea grass grows on the
ocean floor in shallow water.

Living Together

Ocean animals eat plants and other animals. Ocean plants shelter ocean animals. The ocean is full of life.

Glossary

fin—a body part of a fish that is shaped like a flap; fins can be on the fish's back, side, belly or tail; fish use fins to swim and to steer.

ocean floor—the bottom of an ocean; the ocean floor is made of rock.

salt water—water with salt and other minerals in it; water in oceans is salt water; salt water is not safe for people to drink.

shallow—not deep

shell—a hard outer covering; crabs have a hard shell; shells protect crabs.

shore—the land along the edge of a body of water

Read More

Gray, Susan Heinrichs. *Oceans.* First Reports. Minneapolis: Compass Point Books, 2001.

Richardson, Adele D. *Oceans.* The Bridgestone Science Library. Mankato, Minn.: Bridgestone Books, 2001.

Trumbauer, Lisa. *What Are Oceans?* Earth Features. Mankato, Minn.: Pebble Books, 2002.

Internet Sites

Do you want to find out more about oceans?
Let FactHound, our fact-finding hound dog, do the research for you.

Here's how:

1) Visit *http://www.facthound.com*

2) Type in the **Book ID** number: **073682099X**

3) Click on **FETCH IT**.

FactHound will fetch Internet sites picked by our editors just for you!

Index/Word List